*Also by August Kleinzahler*

EARTHQUAKE WEATHER

STORM OVER HACKENSACK

LIKE CITIES, LIKE STORMS

# RED SAUCE,

# WHISKEY AND

# SNOW

*August Kleinzahler*

# RED SAUCE,

# WHISKEY AND

# SNOW

[ *Farrar, Straus & Giroux, New York* ]

Library of Congress Cataloging-in-Publication Data
Kleinzahler, August.
Red sauce, whiskey and snow / August Kleinzahler. — 1st ed.
p.   cm.
I. Title.
PR9199.3.K482W48   1995      811'.54—dc20                    94-24437   CIP

Some of these poems first appeared in the following magazines:
American Poetry Review, Brief, The Bulletin, Carbuncle, Epoch, Giants Play
Well in the Drizzle, Grand Street, Harper's, New American Writing, The New
Yorker, The New York Times, Origin, The Paris Review, PN Review, Poetry,
Scripsi, Sport, Sulfur, The Threepenny Review, and ZYZZYVA.
"Poem" appeared as a broadside issued by Carroll's Books in San Francisco,
1991.
Several of these poems appeared in the Norton collection Postmodern
American Poetry (1994) and in Walk on the Wild Side: Urban American
Poetry Since 1975 (Scribner's, 1994).
The author wishes to thank the John Simon Guggenheim Foundation and the
Lila Wallace-Reader's Digest Fund for their generous assistance.

*To my mother and father*

# *Contents*

**I**

3 / Land's End

5 / The Park

7 / The Wind in March

9 / Rubble

11 / Disclosures

12 / After Catullus

14 / A Glass of Claret
on a Difficult Morning

16 / As the World Turns

17 / The Damselfly

18 / The Festival

19 / Poem

21 / Peaches in November

22 / Cat in Late Autumn

23 / A Case in Point

25 / Song

26 / The Year of the Key

27 / Winter Ball

29 / Crunching Numbers

31 / Dream Juice

32 / East of the Library, Across from
the Odd Fellows Building

34 / Heebie-Jeebies

36 / Jump Tune

38 / Spring Trances

40 / Reno

41 / Reno: Hard-Boiled

44 / Flynn's End

47 / Visits

**II**

51 / San Francisco / New York

53 / Late Winter Morning on the Palisades

54 / Who Stole the Horses from the Indians?

56 / Follain's Paris

60 / Pageant: Rue de Rivoli

62 / Poem Beginning with a Fragment
from Bartleby the Scrivener

64 / A Valentine

65 / Going

67 / The Old Schoolyard in August

68 / Outside the Restaurant

70 / Rooms

72 / Watching Dogwood Blossoms Fall
in a Parking Lot off Route 46

73 / Two Canadian Landscapes

75 / A Fable

77 / Aubade on East 12th Street

78 / Bruce Richard's Trip Down

83 / Pieces of Summer

85 / Sapphics in Traffic

86 / Ruined Histories

87 / A Small Lament

89 / The Porcelain Ink-Boat

90 / Red Sauce, Whiskey and Snow:
A Still Life on Two Moving Panels

92 / Sunday, Across the Tasman

94 / Green River Cemetery: Springs

*So my life was just that way, to keep out of trouble, drink my little whiskey, an' go an' do little ugly things like that, but in a cue-tee way.*

HERMAN E. JOHNSON
*Louisiana blues man*

# PART ONE

# Land's End

*This air,*
you say, *feels as if it hasn't touched land
for a thousand miles,*

as surf sound washes through scrub
and eucalyptus,
whether ocean or wind in the trees

or both: the park's big windmill
turning overhead
while joggers circle the ball field

only a few yards off
this path secreted in growth and mist,
the feel of a long narrow theater set

about it here on the park's western edge
just in from the highway
then the moody swells of the Pacific.

The way the chill goes out of us
and the sweat comes up
as we drive back into the heat

and how I need to take you
to all the special places, or show
you where the fog rolls down

and breaks apart in these hills or where
that gorgeous little piano bridge
comes halfway through the song,

because when what has become dormant,
meager or hardened
passes through the electric

of you, the fugitive scattered pieces
are called back to their nature—
light pouring through muslin

in a strange, bare room.

# The Park

Jimmy the Lush,
looking rough in the shadows and dapple
of light, stares down at the ground
as his dogs take command

of the boundaries,
nuzzling turds and the air around,
snouts jerking like marionettes.
He starts off slow,

nursing a Pepsi, and keeps to his post
through the morning.
He looks almost natty, frayed Ivy League,
compared with the guys

on the corner, wasted already and screaming
about which one goes
to the Arab's next to buy more beer
and some smokes.

Then comes The Talker,
muttering softly, who finds his spot
under the loquat
and fretfully grooms in the shade.

His hat could be a military beret,
but it's far too big

and he wears it wrong, puffed
high on his head like a derby

collapsed at the edges.
They usually detonate round about two,
Jimmy first, somehow
being the senior. A pint's in him now,

high-test, and he's sore
as the dickens about something.
Once it was the mayor, once the Jews,
now it's the whole stinking planet.

The sun posts west
of the radio tower and The Talker's off
on his *possessed by space-villain X* routine,
flogging his rotors, up on his feet,

while Jimmy rails on about the ozone,
the redwoods—those bastards . . .
He spits out the *ba* sound in *bastards*,
his voice growing louder

as his breaths get short
till there's one final shriek

and then silence.

# The Wind in March

*Tower of Texas is spurned for Defense:*
a drunkard and womanizer they say of him,
a mean little man.

And a wild March wind cuts a trough
through the grass, scattering
papers, making the old palmetto weave as tourists,

shoppers and the homeless pull up their collars,
bending into the wind, pausing an instant
as if to take measure of their gravity before going on.

One after another the headline stories are played out for us,
character and event receding
into a gray, ghostly midden dreams bubble up from

years later, dreams
from which we're awakened by the wind
spraying rain against glass, rattling

the windows in their frames. —*March*,
you think to yourself, trying
to remember the oddly formal little man with a drink

staring at your old girlfriend Lu
with a terrifically stagy, silent-movie sort of leer.
You were about to speak up

when the shudder and knock of wood and glass
brought you awake;
and you lie there for what seems a long time

listening to the wind, forgetting
for a minute who it is with her back pressed
against the length of you,

breathing softly.

# Rubble

**I**

The big claw takes its angle
and drives down hard,
shivering Kezar's concrete bleachers

raises up and drops again,
half a section crumbling into rubble

> *McElhenny shakes a tackle,*
> *cuts back hard against the grain,*
> *returning a punt for six*

A thirty-year-old TV clip
stirring the mind's phosphors
as the claw slams down one final time—

a scatback's moves flickering in amber


**II**

After the big shake chimney rubble
at the foot of the block,
and tributaries of Amaretto and Schlitz
winding through broken glass
outside the liquor shop

Then sirens
and the sky full of helicopters circling
the vast smoking feed

Two days of soft weather
and now rain
soaking poppies and sweet alyssum, jasmine
blooming along the fence
where we'd woven its shoots all summer

The old hippie will be back
with the sun, used albums fanned out
in front of the deli,
and the garbage truck will wake us at dawn,
men slamming down cans and cursing

But the earth continues to wobble,
and the cat keeps to his odd new perch
on top of the mantel,
that same fierce look in his eyes

You're figuring it out, one
bit after another,
as each veil
drops to earth like a leaf.

This is the lupine shoot,
this the weed,
this the love withheld,
and here,
          half a life after,
where the trigger's
·released.

The pattern discloses itself,
the dance,
             insect-simple:

appetite, decay,
          growl and suck.

# After Catullus

*(For Thom Gunn on the occasion of his sixtieth birthday)*

Heyho, loverboy
is that a radioactive isotope you've got
burning through your shirtfront
or are you just glad to see me?

       Chump—
you couldn't bear it at her age
much less now.
Had you supposed the years made you pliant?
Look at yourself,

flesh hanging off you
same as the old fucks you take steam with
at the gym.
Better lay off the piss, buddyboy.

Think she doesn't notice?
She sees plenty.
Ask her girlfriends. Ask the hard-bellied punks
she has it off with in the dark.

Why don't you stop licking your nuts in the corner
like an injured tom.
And quit muttering.
You knew what you were up to

when you got into this.
All of your ex-sweethearts are arranged in a chorus,
each in a pinafore with dazzling florets,
laughing themselves sick.

The snip-snap worm has made eggs
and worse
      in the night
six crucial bolts spent their threads
holding fast
your cargo of antibodies.

Spirochetes drop from the rafters
with the poise of hawks.
Your crop of jellybabies is lost.

As you round the Horn, denied
all succor, not
scurvy grass, not even ale

remember what the Captain said
off the coast of St. Lupe,
his face raddled from port:


*Across the dish of the world,*
*from the broccoli and squab*
*to the mysterious chowders*

*keep your bib snapped tight*
*and no stain will come*
*to your peregrine shirt.*

*If breached, hie to land*
*and wait for the chamomile.*
*Meanwhile, eat light, swim*

*close to shore*
*and steer clear of the locals.*

## As the World Turns

**I**

      darling, friends
fly off it and up the flue—astronauts
with their umbilicals cut—
intoning as they go
a refrain that sounds awfully . . . Well,

those fearsome bugs that dwell in cracks
eat beams
from the inside out and *TIMBER*:
another glad idea turns into a rum TV show
avaricious weenie boys and girls

suck right in.

**II**

The deejay in the booth upstairs keeps
slamming them back
with the same round of songs, songs
they didn't like new;

but they're dancing anyhow, faces gone
pale from the noise,
moving their hips
through a long, fretful hunt for the beat.

# The Damselfly

A petal of jasmine caught up
by the breeze
or morning glory aflutter
between the four o'clock and naked lady?

No, not a flower at all,
a butterfly,
showing suddenly white
against the green of a leaf.

And that blue there, cobalt
a moment, then iridescent,
fragile as a lady's pin
hovering above the nasturtium?

*Ah*, the older poet tells me,
*that's a damselfly.*

*And if you just slowed down
and* looked,
*you'd see all sorts of things—*

midmorning toward the end of summer,
head swimming in the garden's perfume

after a quick, surprise rain.

A B-52 bomber from out near Sacramento
is up there somewhere
with a forlorn pilot or loose bolt
ready to plunge
through what the weatherman likes to call
*low coastal cloud* or *the marine layer*.

Keep watching.
Here below, the bandleader calls out,
—*Are we having a good time?*

You bet.
                    Her shoulder's
silk.
Let's have a lick. Yum,
salt's what helps make atoms meet.

Meet too
this little parade of hydrocephalics
the Foundation loves
to trot out for one last stab
at a dance in the sun.

Sure we've got rituals,
trusty as the gears and cogs of ancient clocks,
the innards all exposed
and turning.

She's flipping like a marlin
in lamplight, the air above her
thrashed to a foam

that eddies awhile
and then drifts down to crackle
and glow on her belly.

The one eye's wild
with three shrieks inside it,
the other adrift in a vapor.

Her breathing's chased
with tiny, disembodied cries
percolating

to her lips from another place;
and *click*:
the reel switches to fast-forward,

whistling through her head.
She goes slack,
taken by an undertow

until *click*: a string
of broken snarls, cloacal, a necklace
strung with shards,

then a great heaving, her body
arched toward some lodestar—

and she's released.

## Peaches in November

Peaches redden,
and at day's end glow as if lit from within
the way bronze does,

before thudding down.
Mourning doves scatter at the sound,
shooting away in low trajectories,

and the mind starts
in spite of itself, even after weeks
of hearing them drop through the night

and all day long;
the intervals so far off any possible grid
of anticipation, and the impact

each time they hit
ground amid a racket of leaves
just different enough

from the time before,
and the time before that, you are tricked
out of thought, awake

to the sound
as the last of them come down
and the boughs slowly raise themselves up.

Minou sleeps all day. Old
      soldiers with bum radios
stuck in downtown residence hotels
      see more light
than Minou.
         Sundays,
when rain streams off fire escapes,
      plunging into alleys,
and what little is left of light
      on the street comes off
olive oil cans from Lucca and the groves
      near Córdoba
in a window with pears, dish soap
      and nuts, Minou
looks nearly dead, a forepaw draped on top
      of his head. He's way
out there, sunk deep
      in the textured rayon
of a buff-colored cushion. His whiskers'
      occasional twitch: you see
the heart jump in his fur
      as he stalks the perimeter
of an enormous dream, rain
      turning so heavy near dusk
night slips in
      without you even noticing.

# A Case in Point

Because he's lost the way to his pulse
and doesn't know how to get back.
He bips when he ought to bop,
so now can't do any better than that.

Because even if he knew how
there's nothing in his head or heart
to drive it down the track,
just the corrosive white noise of anxiety,

a sort of ether
coursing through rancor and cunning.

Because he is flummoxed by the world,
the crush of it, the variety.
Too daunted to field what he might,
takes refuge in a text
of a text,
            finding *tickle points of nyceness*
there to stay him.

Because he is a team player, a flak
for the ward boss, the whiffling panjandrums,
backing off from the authentic
like a jackal from the lion's scent.

Because he honors not the made thing
nor can he recognize it when coming upon it.

And yet, should it declare itself
with such force as to penetrate even this,

he averts his eyes and hurries off.

You keep poking at it
finger, drill, snout and awl
till you find yourself at the back
    of the shed
flush against some wall

Sing the song of homing
sing it once more
    con brio
as the bright wind whips
the banners and shiny foil

    *—Are you an* Ex-is-ten-tial-ist,
*Mr. Mister?*

    *—Oh, no, no,*
*I would prefer to think*

*of myself, ahem,*
*as a* Collision-Ecstasist.

    *—You undress on impact,*
*sir?*

    *—Oh, hohohoho,*
*not no more.*

23.5 seconds
for the knurled carbide blade
to pass
twice, tip to bow
and back
biting its cuts in a spray of brass

while the others drop pins
or shim them out
talking pensions, the ball game
and cars:
   *Another ten years, man*
*and I'm gonna* live . . .

and you gauge the next blank
in the basement
behind the transformer
light like a drug mart's
they want you out of
in 23.5 seconds

purchase and all
'ceptin' you, guy
you, staring at the clock

this is where you *live*

The squat man under the hoop
throws in short hooks, left-handed, right
in the dwindling sunlight as six lesbians
clown and shoot at the other end,
through a very loose game of three on three.

How pleased to be among themselves,
warm New Year's Day afternoon, neither young
nor graceful nor really good shots
but happy for the moment while a mutt
belonging to one of them runs

nearly out of its skin so glad to be
near the action and smells, vigorous and dumb
but keeping his orbits well-clear of the man
who would be a machine now if he could,
angling them in off both sides of the backboard.

You can tell this is a thing he's often done,
the boy who'd shoot till dusk
when starlings exploded, filthy birds,
from roost to roost, gathering only to fly off
at the first sharp sound, hundreds as one.

He'd wonder where they went at night
as he played his solitary game of *Round the World*,
sinking shots from along the perimeter,

then the lay-up, then the foul.
                              So intent at it
and grave it almost seemed like more than a game
with dark coming on and the cold.

Assault    plasma    star    launch
*The muezzin's call to prayer*    anthrax    Apache    raid
Slam    mangroves    duel    ranger    excel
*Its delicate, wavering airs*    skewer    rocket    Nintendo
Hunt    rapiers    stun    flaming debris
Blister agents    propel    foxbats    *so delicate the hour before dawn*
Mirage    strafes    laser turbo    fury
Reactor vessels    boil-in-the-bag    lacquered&flaked with gold
*It resembles no other music*    Raytheon    swing-wing
Have-Nap Popeye    punch through    date groves    coral reefs
The silkworm takes a direct hit
*Unless perhaps the nightingale*    turret    spray    leopard    berms
Glancing blow    *in lands where nightingales*
Rain down    bouncing betty    red, Tru-spokes, louvers&air
*Seldom are heard*    pestle&waterwheel    kick ass
Copper flasks of rosewater    grip    sidewinders    grunts
In the iwan's shadows    *triggering the failure*
*Of Asian monsoons*    wild weasel    *all mud and blood down there*
Thiodiglycol    topple    Aries    denial
*Come gargling from froth-corrupted lungs*    the heron turns
To grab hold of the cloud passing by
Storage tanks full of butane    sherbet    positions Hezbollah
Lozenges of basbousa and baklava    strike package
Lynx    impala    *one morning a carpenter's pet monkey*    centrifuged
Cormorants, sea cows and terns    with light
Collateral damage    crushed mint    rewarded his generals
*With duck farms and Mercedes*    uranium hexafluoride

Scented with myrrh     the lion leapt onto the gazelle's back
          Tearing his neck     blanched almonds     attrite
How watered silk took the calligrapher's ink     cut off     flotilla
          Rake     minaret     thin slices of roast kid
Basted with pomegranate     MiGs in the dust of Nineveh, at the gates of Ur
          *There was once a certain venerable dervish*
Jaguars     sirens     titanium-tipped     tracers     *caused the market*
          *To rebound on news of the successful bombing*
Saffron gathered from fields of crocus     alert     mosaics
          Sunday has been designated     baby milk
                    Phantoms     in flames
                         Azan

Peg, bolt the door quick
*Fatty waste*　　　　　　　*gasoline cans*
A tiger's in the kitchen
Shoulder-high to the counter
Licking the paint off
What a stench
*Gland burgers*　　　　　　*excrement*
If it's a dream
Give the projector a flip, willya
Please
Get under the covers
(Uh-oh, the transom)
He's smearing
Stripes all over the stereo
And up along the wainscoting
Geez
If he roars, what
Call the fire truck
He'll blow the house down
And freak the kids
Is Paddy safe
*Whisker*　　　　　　　　*marmot*
He seems benign enough
But look
The flashlight's broke
Now his drool's getting onto the burners
Try Dr. Sam
Oh balls, it's Veterans Day

## East of the Library, Across from the Odd Fellows Building

That bummy smell you meet
off the escalator at Civic Center, right before
you turn onto McAllister,
seems to dwell there, disembodied,
on a shelf above the sidewalk.

The mad old lady with lizard skin
bent double
         over her shopping cart
and trailing a cloud of pigeons
is nowhere in sight.

A pile of rags here and there
but no one underneath.
         An invisible shrine
commemorating what?
Old mattresses and dusty flesh,

piss and puked-on overcoats, what?
         Maybe death,
now there's a smell that likes to stick around.
You used to find it in downtown Sally Anns
and once

in a hospital cafeteria, only faintly,
after a bite of poundcake.
         But here it lives,

cheek by jowl with McDonald's,
still robust after a night of wind

with its own dark little *howdy-do*
for the drunks and cops,
social workers and whores,
or the elderly couple from Zurich
leafing cooly through their guidebook.

Now he's Daruma, now he's Swifty,
hands pressed together in pious concern
for all sentient beings, the snares
of desire,
         while his mind in a froth
reckons angles, exits and a safe spot to hide.

His face furrows from the inside out.
The arduousness of it all,
intent and appearance at cross-purposes.
Poor guy, you'd think he was on the ropes
the way he covers and ducks,

Macho Camacho digging at his kidneys.
But no one takes any notice
except for a concerned old pen pal and a tired wife.
Caught up with him the other day
outside the zendo

just after morning prayers, the fog
gone early and the sidewalk smelling
of summer morning.
         *—Looks to be a warm one,*
I said, passing on my way to work.

And he flinched,
eyes darting left and right.

By the look of him a stranger might guess
he'd grabbed some money from a beggar's cup

or got nabbed with his thumb in the pie.

Wake, wake—
Oxalis, wild little buttercups hurt
my eyes after the long dark ride
underground.

         Am I blue? You'd be too,
cobalt, attack blue.


Have a sip of the red gorget
our hummingbird gives a flash of right
above the peach tree's topmost twig
before he cranks his sweets

              and then darts off,
the leaves below rusted by frost.


  *Azzurra, azzurra,*
*la ghiandaia azzurra è rabbiosa.*
(Robbie who, sir?)

         The neighbor's whitewash job
neatly chimes with two white courting butterflies
and that new rear landing's cross rails echo
what?

    Rick, go find a horizontal quick
and give that lady back her apron, too.


I haven't the wind?

         Oh, yes I do,
attack blue. See those bees? No?

In the mimosa's bushy flowers?
So big, fat and eager at it the timid leaflets
swoon.

      But wait a minute, back they come:
spring-driven. Oh,

did you think I'd given up or boiled down
into glue,

         you rascal, you?
Hairy old rhizome keeps cool down low awhile,
then . . .

      Ecce, Ricky, presto:
it's your rank, harum-scarum perennial,
weedy and rude.

Two snails have found the inside of a Granny Goose
Hawaiian-style potato chips,
the clipper ship on its wrapper
headed out from the islands

on a wind-swept main.
The last storms passed now, turning
to snow in the High Sierra:
they baste in their ointments deep in the tall grass,

cool among shadows and cellophane.
The sparrows and linnets have gone mad at dawn,
trilling and swooping in the branches
and ditchweed, flashing a plume

then diving; a racket
we've woken to for weeks, far too long
before the sun turns Scotch broom and the poppies to flame.
We drift through these days

half in trance from fatigue.
At evening, as the streaks of light dissolve,
we watch the boy walk home,
hatband and uniform wet from the game.

The smell of dust and sweat and the oil in his mitt
burns deep into the tissue of him.

Buffeted, drunk, wounded—
his pretty nerves bloom,

a school of minnows just under the skin.
The wind carries music up from the street,
a skewer running through him
that he slowly turns on in the scented dark.

Along the Truckee
in the dawn cool, a few blocks west
of the *good morning dears* in white sweaters
smoking fast,
you can watch light come into the crests
of the mountains
and water sluice over the spillways and weir
onto granite boulders.

They pull cherries, bells and oranges
under recessed lighting, letting
the ash go
till it drops.
—*She can't even beat up Zasu Pitts,*
*for Chrissakes.*

It's a few hours yet
until the heat and bus-tour caravans
disgorge their cargo
with shiny patterned leisurewear
and cartoon buttocks.

The Southern Pacific rattles by,
three locomotives pulling a mile of cars
while blasted old cowboys
and younger drunks, resembling porn stars,
drift wraithlike past the hotel pools.

# Reno: Hard-Boiled

*(For Geoffrey O'Brien)*

The RVs parked in the Comstock lot radiated heat,
waves of it.
   *Reminds me of El Centro*, Gladys said.
*One June it was so hot you could only pick up two stations*
*on the radio.*
    But south of town you could still make out patches
of snow on the higher peaks over toward Steamboat and Virginia
  City.

Gladys had the sort of face that belongs in magazines
where you're not supposed to notice the face.
       The hotel she found us
was one of those old brick affairs with a fancy cornice
and Nevada Gothic in the doors and windows.
Probably elegant once, it now felt more like the backdrop
for a Jim Thompson novel, one that will never be filmed.

The old guy at the front desk was a top classic fit as well
with the cowboy tie, suspenders and tiny white mustache:
dapper, creased and shiny to the tips of his pointy black boots.
Everybody was out of central casting that week,
even the drifters lounging around outside the Mission
or that beat-up little bungalow called House of Hope.
So when Eddie took a shiv in his gut that night
in the parking lot of Mr. D's Backstage Club
we were into the plot, Gladys, the killer and me,
whether we liked it or not.

My life's been a succession of Gladyses, I thought to myself,
watching her pore over the Racing Form hours on end,
smoking Chesterfields in her underwear.
                                        Late afternoons
she'd go catch the feature race at the Sports Parlor
in the Flamingo and commence with the gimlets.
Meanwhile, she might as well have been reading the Talmud
she was so still and engrossed, except when she butted her smokes
on Goofy's snout in the joke ashtray she'd won at some casino.

I found myself on a bar stool later that evening
at Mr. D's next to a curiously solemn Englishman.
He smelled of prime rib, bourbon and sweat and kept sticking
five-spots in the panties of a young blonde who danced
dirty for him while he just sat there and sipped his whiskey.

Between songs you could hear the freeway in the distance.
He was one of those gruff, blocky, northern English,
working-class, who said *ruhf* (as in *bow-wow*) for *rough*.
You'd think he'd never seen a blonde in her knickers before
the way he kept muttering—
                            *Christ, you're buffed*
(rhyming with *ruhf'd*), then something about a *chubby* he had
        *on.*

I decided to go outside and take some fresh air
when I ran into Lois, a high yellow gal from back East.

She was older than the others and used to know Gladys
from their Century 21 days over in Tahoe.
I checked out the giant billboard across the highway
with Sammy Davis and Roy Orbison look-alikes:
something about a forthcoming *Night of Stars.*

Dead stars, seemed like to me.
Lois knew I wasn't there for a couch dance.
Eddie and I go all the way back to lava lamps,
when we ran up and down the coast to Ensenada.
Lois would have been just a scowling kid then,
pitching pennies against a wall in Brooklyn.

The Southern Pacific began roaring past
along the top of a ridge a few blocks behind us,
pulling eighty carloads of coal from Utah.
I suddenly picked up a whiff of her perfume.
It reminded me a little too well of car freshener.
That was an instant before she fell into my arms,
dead as the smoked trout Gladys had for dinner
at the Basque place, along with about seven gimlets,
on an evening that now seemed a lifetime away.

Flynn fell off the cable car
and landed on his head.

                    Poor Flynn,

hardly Flynn anymore,
in a dory listing to starboard.

Flynn on his stool,
holding court down the block
at The Magic Flute,
his hound at his feet while old LPs
hissed and popped through the weekend:

Boccherini and Mississippi Fred,
the plucky chanteuse and gag tunes.

Flynn with his mug of rum
and that faraway gaze—
a wryness at the eyes and mouth
frozen into a carapace
over some enormous hurt.

You see it in the look of old beatniks
at their rituals
in the bar window, solemnly
playing cards at noon,
afflicted with some private wisdom
denied parturition.

Flynn, drunk and alone
in his shop weekday afternoons
with binfuls of concerti
and wailing brass.
                    Alone with his dog
and his rum and the fog
coming in and too stiff
to get up and change the record.

And Flynn with his secret poems
in a fancy red box,
thwarted and feverish and illustrated
by a suburban Beardsley,

whatever ache or shame
prettified, made diffuse and tied
with a rhyme
like a ribbon round a present.

The ghost of him presiding
over those last lost afternoons
weeks after the earthquake,
laths and studs showing through
the walls, and plaster
sprinkling the ancient Vocalions.

A consortium bought the block
and the old place has a new front

with black glass,
very minimal, very flash
and sells computer software.

And Flynn drifts further and further to sea
in his bed at Laguna Honda.

You were speaking of your brother that night,
outside on the landing, the two of us
sharing one last smoke.
               I was headed east
for February and you were hoping to finish your work up here
and make it back to Recife in time for Carnival.

It was very late. The street was quiet and dark.
You talked about him always driving back from town drunk
the fifty or so kilometers along country roads
to the sugarcane farm he ran.
                    What a wonderful driver
he was, sure and alert, even when drinking,
and how well he knew those roads, but still,
one night . . .

             You were beautiful just then,
your face naked, luminous with feeling
for him and the sorrow you sensed in his life,
an adoring trance—
               when I looked up,
and right on top of us the radio tower,
soaring a thousand feet, its red beacon
pulsing across the sky.

I nearly swooned for all the wine and smoke and *feijoada*,
you and Louisa vamping all night to the Cardoso records,

then my head thrown back

to the monstrous surprise of it,
suddenly looming.
I didn't know this neighborhood at night,
or had never bothered to look up.


But that's really it, after all:
like Monsieur Krivine from Lyons, the symphony conductor,
when we walked across town years ago
and admired the skyline from Russian Hill.

*—Magnificent,*

he gasped.
*—You enjoy tall buildings?* I asked.

*—No, no,* he said,

*the shapes they make of the sky.*

# PART TWO

# San Francisco / New York

A red band of light stretches across the west,
low over the sea, as we say goodbye to our friend,
Saturday night, in the room he always keeps unlit
and head off to take in the avenues,
actually take them in, letting the gables,

bay windows and facades impress themselves,
the clay of our brows accepting the forms.
Darkness falls over the district's slow life,
miles of pastel stucco canceled
with its arched doorways and second-floor businesses:

herbalists and accountants, jars
of depilatories. Such a strange calm, the days
lengthening and asparagus already
under two dollars a pound.
                              Is New York fierce?

The wind, I mean. I dream of you in the shadows,
hurt, whimpering. But it's not like that, really,
is it? Lots of taxis and brittle fun.
We pass the shop of used mystery books
with its ferrety customers and proprietress

behind her desk, a swollen arachnid
surrounded by murder and the dried-out glue

of old paperback bindings.
                                What is more touching
than a used-book store on Saturday night,

dowdy clientele haunting the aisles:
the girl with bad skin, the man with a tic,
some chronic ass at the counter giving his art speech?
How utterly provincial and doomed we feel
tonight with the streetcar appearing over the rise

and at our backs the moon full in the east,
lighting the slopes of Mount Diablo
and the charred eucalyptus in the Oakland hills.
Did you see it in the East 60's
or bother to look up for it downtown?

And where would you have found it,
shimmering over Bensonhurst, over Jackson Heights?
It fairly booms down on us tonight
with the sky so clear,
                        and through us

as if these were ruins, as if we were ghosts.

# Late Winter Morning
## on the Palisades

Candle in the throat of maple
alive in wet bark
like a soldering flame as the sun lifts
over Manhattan's shoulder,

the yard for a minute, no more,
washed in an antique gold,
a kind of cathedral light filtering down
on squirrels

digging up turf. The earth,
after a fortnight's thaw,
loosens, loosening some more
until a musty bouquet

digs a small trench in us, light
playing on pebbles and clods,
traceries in clay.
                Suddenly car doors,
jets and *the brutal slaying in Queens*—

morning rinsing the shadows,
pouring out day.

# Who Stole the Horses
# from the Indians?

*Who stole the horses from the Indians?*
my father used to ask.

                                   *Was it you?*

*Oh no!* I'd pipe. *Not me.*
But my father always knew.

Then there was another game:
*Where are you going?*

                           *To China*, I'd announce,
*Asbury Park, Hollywood.*

*Say hello to Dorothy Lamour. Don't forget
to write.*
           And off I'd spring,
but never fast enough.
He'd catch me by the arm and haul me in.

*Where are you going?*
my father used to ask when I was grown.

*Alaska*, I would tell him,
*Lisbon, Montreal.*

                      *You can't,*
my father would tell me.
*Drifters live that way.*

But he was older and I was quick.
*You can't*, he'd say.

                And off I'd go.

*Where are you going?*
my father asks,

             and now he's old.

*Vancouver*, I tell him,
*San Francisco, Idaho.*

He just smiles sadly,
and says hardly anything at all.

I can remember first walking to the city
accompanied by rumors buzzing in the hedgerows.
I made my way past big red villas,
a perfect decor for both the criminal and his victim.

Small children played under carts
while babies in the chestnut's shadows
slept and wet through the afternoon.
There is an abundant peace to be found here

in the blue, then gray and mauve eyes
of the voluptuous women cutting bread into an embossed tureen.

The path to La Courtille has been dug up by pickaxes
but the sky hasn't changed,
tinted by smoke rising from café-restaurants
and the apartments of the rich

with their Belle Epoque furniture,
popular once more with this latest crop of indolents
always chattering about foreign travel
and smoking Turkish cigarettes.
                              As for the factory smoke,
it rises into the same old blue sky of the Middle Ages
the jongleurs and dream-brokers tried to climb.

Literature and life are warming to each other.
At the Botanical Gardens a stiff breeze

arrives with early evening, shaking
the small signs with Latin names on them

that hang half-hidden amid clusters of plants.
What a beautiful night for a philosophical debate!

A man follows the alleyways
back to his flat with its persistent odor
that somehow has survived all the women perfumed
with heliotrope. He inspects the place

until he comes upon his shaving mirror,
spotted with coagulated drops of blood.
He takes off his sweaty shirt
and dust settles in the tufts of his armpits.

Old images possess him
as he lounges on his bed with its peony-colored coverlet
turned down. Images of Flanders and Artois,
the country girl smiling at the miner

who fusses with his Davy lamp.
Images of the Midi and burning walls.

He hasn't forgotten his copies of *Salammbô*,
*Les Odelettes* and *Poèmes saturniens*

stacked on the shelves.
But for now he is preoccupied

with a hole in his sock, and besides,
the books are looking worn.

Later on you may encounter him
walking the pavement of the quai de l'Oise,
watching wrinkles form on the water's surface,
or across the street

moving against a backdrop of brown doors.
He takes an elbow in the ribs
at a busy intersection, and when the north wind
has at him as well

he yearns for spinach and quail fat,
the dark juices of roasts and splendid silverware.

He passes a dilapidated bar with a sign
of a curiously tempered charm
that cost the painter not a little care.
The museum nearby is closed

with its coughs and slow steps,
its canoes, its Aztec mummies and once-poisoned arrows.

While at the Emporium
the feverish shoplifter dips her ringed fingers

into the lingerie.

*(with Deborah Treisman)*

The dark man in the crêpe booth
spreads batter on the grill as the world streams
past the tableau of him, the traffic
and crowds a blur, dappled.
The cop, the professor and poule
are wax. The nervous man, too,
wax, agitated.
              She throws open the shutters
of her tiny room
and the sun strikes her flesh, not
the blow to the chest
Frédéric endured when lamplight exposed
Mme. Arnoux's years,
but a delicate stitching of warmth
along the base of her throat.

In an hour the sky will darken
and rain pour down, spilling from the mouths
of gargoyles.
            The cop, the professor
and poule stand under an awning
with a tour group from Naples and three White
Russians, bickering over Melnikov's
scheme for a car park
held up by caryatids to span the Seine.
The professor scowls, but stylishly.

For now the sun is high,
late morning. The young woman stretches
first one arm then the next.
The Mussulman is in the crêpe booth
with his bananas and jam.

                A day, an epoch—
a sagging lintel, a worn stone step . . .

The world streams past the poule
with her bruised mouth, the cop
peeking from under his hat at her;
the professor in his leather jacket,
his cigarette;
the impassive face in the crêpe booth:

the set darkening
as the breeze picks up and the clouds move in
from the west.

# Poem Beginning with a Fragment
# *from* Bartleby the Scrivener

*A rounded and orbicular sound to it, and rings*
*like unto bullion—*
$\qquad\qquad\qquad$ the description so plagued
Mme. Cornichon's memory as she adjusted her slip
before settling herself onto the furze

for what she hoped would be reverie.
Ants scattered, two large beetles as well,
of such a kind as she had never seen,
enormous, their plates giving off an iridescent sheen

as they scuttled willy-nilly in slow-motion alarm.
Above her, hidden among leaves, the chatter
of wrens and grackles was as a fretful orison
to her in her repose, but the music that ranged

most freely through her being was Ravel's "Miroirs,"
especially so "Oiseaux tristes," suggested by the song
of a blackbird *but in the mood* of a "bird lost
in the overwhelming blackness of a forest

during the hottest hour of summer." Ah,
she remembered being awash with glissandi and arpeggios
in the salon of Princesse Edmonde de Polignac,
one afternoon with the skies outside ready to burst—

and did. But drenched as she was, shoes ruined,
she barely noticed, still so transported

by the tapestry of sound—hypnotized. Regrettably,
she took sick, and yet it was the princess,

not she, who succumbed to a bronchial complaint.
What would ever become of the great stuffed owl
suspended above the divan, the Art Nouveau sideboard
and chinoiserie? Blessedly, the illness was swift.

And the Pavane . . . What was it Ravel himself said
after a too too *adagio* performance years later?
Something about that it was the princess, not
the *Pavane*, that was supposed to be dead.

Tired already or just confused?
Here, let's get rid of this one over here,
     put that there on top of there,
and give ourselves some room.

For what?
For the big white cloud spiring across the river
between the shimmer of a DC-10 and Grant's Tomb.

    *—Nice view,*
says the blonde with a dancer's haunch
and those dear, chewy Jersey vowels.
But the eyes are dull.

        Compared to whose?
Yours, in the dark.

*Por que nao me disse o quanto gostou*
*de minha bunda quando fizemos amor?*

        Because,
I'm swimming underwater
and might drown if I speak.

The old people are dying,
they're falling apart piece by piece
like vintage Studebakers,
but the docs keep pumping diuretics and Prednisone
into them, doing valve jobs,
so it's slow, terribly slow.

They're talking tumor,
they're talking colon and biopsy
over biscuit tortoni and tea.
                              The doctors
are butchers, and as for the kids—
selfish insensitive little shits.

Look at Sinatra and Reagan,
dewlaps trembling in the wee small hours,
glued to *I Love Lucy* reruns
as the Secret Service men doze.
They own cliffs and enormous stretches
of desert, those two—
shopping centers, distilleries.

Lucy is dead, boys, give it up:
Desi, the Duke and Ava,
dust;

even little Sammy's
checked out.

All the great ones, the class acts,
taking their bows
                    or history.

# The Old Schoolyard in August

The welling of cicadas in the green
afternoon before the storm
catches on some inner ratchet along with the leaves
so dark and dense in the fading light
their color washes into surrounding air.

And when the first drops pock the dust
of the ballfield next to the school,
it is not a piercing aria
or iridescent jellyfish parachuting upwards
but darkness

spreading, troweled across the diaphragm.
Every breath drags through it,
bringing in its wake a bewilderment
of fire trucks and galoshes,
the taste of pencils and Louis Bocca's ear

torn off by the fence in a game of *salugi*.

# Outside the Restaurant

My lady pulled my sleeve
to see
     the squat man on the sidewalk
near

hand on his joint,
under siege by terrible gravity

      pulling him down
      pulling him down

blood and phlegm
caked to his chin, meat

of him, liquid
drawn down to the ground

pitiful to behold,
moving
     slowly by us

turned,
galling his bones

turned back to us
and said

acid,
dark as a witch:

—*So long, beautiful.*

In the sleep that finally gives rest
I take the stairs slowly
out past the azalea dell and bison paddock,
out of view from the meadow,

and down through these rooms once more,
this endless house
under the lawns still wet from mist,
the root systems and mulch,

only to find you at a sales counter
arguing with a Russian woman.
Her English is rough but adequate,
your argument well-reasoned, controlled.

You will in the end prevail.
The salesclerk is charmed by the snatches of Russian
you mix into your conversation,
the garment exchanged for credit.

I seldom find you in these rooms anymore,
certainly not for months.
So when our eyes meet
you look momentarily bemused,

the shiver of surprise softening to pleasure.
You are lovely,

somewhat older than I remember,
businesslike in a tailored suit.

Our conversation is courtly,
flirtatious in what we imagine an Old World way.
How strange to encounter you here
in this harsh light, the tableau

of a downtown department store with its cases
of perfumes, gels and leather goods.
And how inexplicably refreshed I feel afterwards
lying here alone,

awakened precisely as our commerce ended
by the shouts of children going to school.

# Watching Dogwood Blossoms Fall
# in a Parking Lot off Route 46

Dogwood blossoms drift down at evening
        as semis pound past Phoenix Seafood

and the Savarin plant, west to the Turnpike,
        Paterson or hills beyond.

The adulterated, pearly light and bleak perfume
        of benzene and exhaust

make this solitary tree and the last of its bloom
        as stirring somehow after another day

at the hospital with Mother and the ashen old ladies
        lost to TV reruns flickering overhead

as that shower of peach blossoms Tu Fu watched
        fall on the riverbank

from the shadows of the Jade Pavilion,
        while ghosts and the music

of yellow orioles found out the seam of him
        and slowly cut along it.

# Two Canadian Landscapes

**I**

And so Diana visited a tavern called Diana
on a night the wind hurt most.
Her three curs pawed and sniffed the filthy snow;
their red lop ears looked sore in the neon glow.

Shoulder to heel and the span of her filled the door.
Her hurdler's thighs were taut.
Among mortal women only the char is allowed in,
then, after hours, not with a bow but a mop.

Yet here stood the virgin, adored by a treacherous god.
The pool game ceased.
Above her breasts three small tattoos:

    a stag            a date palm         and a bee.

No beer was forthcoming.
Out of her quiver she drew an arrow
with a shaft of silver, feathered crimson and gold.
She sent it the bar's full length.

A quart of lager burst at the neck.
Outside, her hounds snapped smoke.
The great cross shone from the highest hill in town.
Above that, the moon.

**II**

Warm night fog and the smell of pulp
on the wind
          as mill lights in the distance
flicker, fitfully as stars.
Close on March
after the season of rains, front
upon front drubbing cove, spit and seawall,
even crows scarce,
forsaking their perches
when the tumbling sea shook a great fir log
from its sandy notch.
               The mind flutters,
aloft on contrary winds
that pull together skies and then tear them apart.
             Crocuses
in thick husks inch up.
Clusters of them advance as the shank of winter
retreats inland.
           The rain
begins falling again, softly,
an occasional foghorn,
cats' nimble couplings on wet grass:
                        spy
in a strange city—
spring.

# A Fable

Weasel and the Ponce were having a confab
      under the chinaberry tree,
in the shade of the dusty old tree—
      pious Weasel, indefatigable Ponce.

Abroad in the land were pickings to be had,
      marks beyond measure,
fat aplenty for tooth and hand. Will and cunning
      are the clean, bright edges

of a creature in the wild, of a vigorous man,
      so that goodness finds sustenance,
charity nurture, in quietude, in quietude within.
      The nose will relate to you a world,

a world entire, from the merest trace of wind—
      the topography of weakness,
gold in a river's sand. And there they sniffed,
      sniffed and with hooded eye conspired,

in the shadows thrown by the dusty old tree.
      Trading knowledge, whetting tools,
they made ready for their necessary enterprise,
      the fate nature bestowed. All the while

drinking in each other's aspect: they found
      uncommon pleasure there,

did Weasel and his friend, in the other's smile and guise,
       as a young girl in flattering light,

as a darling young girl by her reflection might—
       the two of them, lovely beyond compare
in the shade of the chinaberry tree.
       Groomed, laved with blandishment,

almost gilded in the hours afternoon turns to evening
       and evening, stealthily, to night,
how would they have noticed the rustle in the thicket,
       felt the heat of its burning eyes?

# Aubade on East 12th Street

The skylight silvers
and a faint shudder from the underground
travels up the building's steel.

Dawn breaks across this wilderness
of roofs with their old wooden storage tanks
and caps of louvered cowlings

moving in the wind. Your back,
raised hip and thigh
well-tooled as a rounded baluster

on a lathe of shadow and light.

# Bruce Richard's Trip Down

So I buy a pig in a poke and sign on.
One thing I did know, it was a Hans Christian 38,
cutter-rigged with a big, old-fashioned, full keel,
about four and a half tons of it, which meant
whatever came our way we wouldn't be sinking anyhow.

Stan, the skipper, didn't have a lot to say
but I got a good feel out of him.
The other hand, Lowell, was a librarian
and right off strikes me as a dilettante.
He's read books, OK, and talks good nautical
but has a fat ass, and that raises a few questions.

We head out of Bellingham around ten in fog.
It's Labor Day Monday and, Jesus, the strait's filled
with pleasure craft trying to make Deception Pass
at slack water, a real narrow little shot
between Whidbey and Fidalgo Islands.
You can see the charter boats poke through the fog

as we make our way slowly among them and west
to the ocean, hugging the coast, three or four miles
off the Olympic Peninsula. The fog lifts
and all of a sudden there are those peaks
shooting up like to make your head swim. At 3
a.m. we make Cape Flattery, the far edge

of the continent, and steer to the open sea.
Next day we're into blue water, "blue water sailors."

Lord-O-Dear, it's pretty: clear, no debris,
no logs or kelp, no birds; maybe an albatross
and a couple of gray whales up close, pretty pretty blue.

Out a hundred miles, free of the shipping lanes,
we point south and pick up a northerly
on our stern. What we wanted was for the wind
to be on our beam, giving us a bit of speed
and lift, instead of a wind like this,
bagging the sails and making for lots of roll,

which puts me off my chow and keeps me that way.
The wind picks up to 20 knots on the fifth day
and the boat really starts rockin' and rollin'
in this harmonic motion you fight with the wheel.

But we've begun making time and head into the night
with the headsails up. By now we are well along,
maybe on line with Port Orford and The Heads
down the Oregon coast and the wind picking up steady.

Me and Stan trade two-hour shifts with the wind
gusting to 25. We turn on the deck lights
and drop the big headsail. All we have left
is the storm jib off the starboard with the wind
still dead north and increasing as we point due south.
Lowell's down below, which is right where we want him.

In the cockpit it feels like you're going 60
what with the wind and white water racing past
your ears when it's only 4, 4½ knots you're traveling.
Your senses play tricks on you about now,
fixed on the red dial of the compass, fighting off sleep,
only 10° to play with either side of downwind.

When you look forward you see the headsail silhouetted
against the sky, floating, like a wing in a dream.
Meanwhile, you're busy trying to pop the wheel
against each roll, and you don't want to lose the course
on a turn to port or the boat'll head to weather,
and if you're flat unlucky maybe broach.

When it finally turned light, not much after six,
you could see the waves, huge, forty-footers,
an unbelievable sight, white everywhere,
big graybeards with the wind blowing their tops
into spray. I make up my mind to heave to:
so I throw the wheel all the way over and lock it,
figuring the boat would hold a pretty good course

with the jib back-winded, riding over the tops of waves.
We were headed west now in a full gale
with the wind steady between 35 and 40,
or gusting to 45. I went below to rest,

but at 2 a.m. the boat got caught on the face
of a haystack, an enormous wave, forty foot
from crest to trough, and took a terrible shot
flat on its side, *BAM*. Whoa boy, that puckered my sphincter
and drove the cold wind of wrath down my corridor;
but all that keel weight went right under
and forced the rig back up: winch handles, half
the storm dodger lost; books, tools, kerosene . . .

Next day, the seventh, with the staysail back up,
the skipper decides to abandon the trough
and head south with the wind. By that night
the waves are quieter and farther apart
and we're able to turn around onto a reach
and limp our way in the direction of shore.

We raised a ship the next morning, a freighter
headed east from the Orient. They told us
we were a hundred miles farther south than we thought,
and seventy miles farther west. Stan had had us
dead-reckoned about level with Cape Mendocino.

That's where our luck began. We came round on a beam reach
that brought us all the way to San Francisco.
We wound up sailing past the Farallons just around sunset
and through the Golden Gate into Richmond Bay.
Man, that's a magical feeling, sailing under that bridge

with those big standing waves either side of you,
same as you find sometimes in white-water rapids.

The wind held strong all the way in to Sausalito
where we got the sails down, fired the engine
for anchoring, had us each a couple of beers,
and that's when I phoned you, cousin.

Under the tailings and slag
the salts burn down,
through clay, through schist

and boil in the stream
where the little lamb drinks
slaughtered for meat

that Baby Dee eats
with her sticky green jam
and roast potatoes

●

On the subway escalator,
eyes averted,
pants snug as the skin of half-ripe pears

In pastel rooms all through this melting world
love-thoughts, like cuttings,
have begun to take

●

Car alarms, horns and shouts blend
into a river of sound, muffled
as the sun sets in a final, mescaline cloud

He is close now.
Your nerve ends bristle, as if touched
by the vibrations of an invisible cello

●

Peonies brighter than bees
thrive behind pickets, sunflowers too,
the great heads propped by stakes

Late, when mopeds cool
and flinty shrieks dissolve in the breeze
families sleep in damp underthings

and tomatoes soften on the shelf

●

A man on the front stoop
crying in the middle of the night:

    *—Somebody, please . . .*

The cat lifts his head from sleep,
first toward the voice

        then to me

# Sapphics in Traffic

Festinating rhythm's bothered her axis.
Wobbly on her pins, both her partners grab at
air and stumble, a bit of ad-lib rumpus
　　　tweaking the priggish.

Madame Nostropova, unhinged, cries *Nudna!*
But the problem's in the pit. Check the fiddler
with the bow tie gazing up at Katya, panicked,
　　　lunging at random.

How he longs to crush her, his little Pucci-
nella . . . Now his tempo's about to rocket.
Paganini-esque cadenzas fetch bravos,
　　　driving him, heedless,

onward. Scores are meant for sheep, not for lovers.
She can hear your strings in their frenzied crying.
See her body drawn toward your violin's straining—
　　　yearning in concert.

# Ruined Histories

You so love these photographs, too well perhaps,
and rush to frame the moment, press the shutter,
and get along with this dollhouse saga
you had rehearsed before it ever came to be.

Ah, Little Girl Destiny, it's sprung a leak
and the margins are bleeding themselves away.
You and I and the vase and stars won't stay still.
Wild, wild, wild—kudzu's choked the topiary.

Looks like your history is about to turn
random and brutal, much as an inch of soil or duchy.
Not at all that curious hybrid you had in mind:
Jane Austen, high-tech and a measure of Mom.

You're lost, desolate as Savannah after Sherman.
The lavender sachet, marbled storybooks,
the ring Grandma left you, poor Damien's love letters . . .
It's just your eyes, ass, me and a broken Nikon.

# A Small Lament

*Mafaleeta*                    *Coulo*

    *Vongule*

        *Ti Ketta*

Awns and wild chicory

The first autumn in ten the peach tree didn't bear

Asleep in the mallow and rye grass

In a pool of shadows

The left ear swivels, something on the wind

Or a flea

One eye half-open, solemn as an old gator in the weeds

This strange quiet now, darkness on the landing, a far-off cry

After the harmonics and stops

Raised in your syrinx, the abundance of tunes

Savage or beguiling

That earth smell, fresh, deep in the fur of you

One paw on my darling's breast, gazing up at her

Into her eyes

With his coarse tongue licks the salt off her flesh

Fitful *Pockateeka*

No children or foxtails to trouble your rest

A wedge of light, extirpated

The music of you, bleeding into the soil

With the leaves and spores and gases, vibrating awhile

But you waited, you waited until I was right

Just another pretty morning in May

*Falla*

    *Nanj*

        my sweet, sweet boy

# The Porcelain Ink-Boat

The dragon and phoenix are swept along with the clouds
over wave-washed rocks and across the white bow,
drawn in a blue mortared only at the kilns of Ching-te-Chen—
*absence of repose.*
                       The old riverboat itself tossing
in a stiff wind as it floats along the Chang
with its cargo of ewers, stem cups and bowls

and continues its journey across the Poyang Lake
to Chinkiang and then by Grand Canal to Tientsin,
down the Pei Ho River, finally to Beijing.
And it is to the west of that thronging capital
that the poet dips his brush into the boat
now abrim with ink, lightly scented,
and composed as the Mo Ching recommends

with a mixture of pine soot and glue
either from deer horn or the skin of carps,
attending with his brushwork to a dream
now many weeks old but which haunts him still
of an acorn falling from a solitary oak,

not to the image of acorn or oak but to the spirit
that dwells in the instant before it hits ground.

# Red Sauce, Whiskey and Snow:
# A Still Life on Two Moving Panels

Ingots of cinnabar and gold

Under a window of snow

Snow-sky, ganglia of dark branches claw up at it

Olive-skinned Tina soaks in the tub

Snow along the Hudson, fastening to stone the length of the
Palisades

Falling on valleys and abandoned pavilions at the river's northern
reaches

The kitchen light almost amber, Dutch Interior light

The little green vase, stone Buddha and indigo cat, backlit on
the windowsill

Through the window wild diagonals of snow

Blowing across planes of snow

Gables and sweeping roofs, shadows, brick and an enormous crow

Sponging her swarthy aureoles small vesicles appear

The ferry slips through the snow, back and forth to Manhattan

The towers ghostly as it pulls away from shore

A gathering aroma of earth and fruit

As the sauce darkens with the juices of meat, craters and thickens

Somewhere back there, early in the second movement

The clarinet located an emotion, one long forgotten

Then let it go

Drifts have nearly buried the pumphouse

And a great quiet has covered the swings and jungle gym

The suave bite of oak, an unfastening, a tap at the base of the
skull

The slow release of sibilants, *o*'s and *l*'s

Then thunder, muffled, snow thunder, no

A big jet passing by low, hidden in cloud

# Sunday, Across the Tasman

Big weather is moving over the headlands.
Turrets and steeples jab up at it
and the bank towers stand rooted,
logos ablaze at the edge of the earth.

In a suburban church basement the AA faithful
are singing hymns of renewal, devotion
and praise. He struggles with his umbrella
in the lobby of the Art Deco theater,

a dead ringer for the old 72nd Street Loew's
with its plaster Buddhas and kitsch arabesques—
the Preservation Society's last, best stand.
Young couples walk past hand in hand

as golden oldies flood onto the sidewalk
from the sweatshirt emporium next door.
His heart bobs, a small craft
awash for a moment with nostalgia.

Bartok liked to pick out a folk melody
and set it, a jewel in the thick
of hammered discords and shifting registers:
not unlike this dippy Mamas and Papas tune

floating along nicely among the debris.
The rain turns heavy, and the first

of the night's wild southerlies keens through,
laying waste the camellia and toi toi.

He wonders how the islanders managed
in their outriggers: if they flipped
or rode it through, plunging
from trough to trough with their ballast

of hoki, maomao, cod. Time for a drink.
A feral little businessman shakes
the bartender's left breast in greeting,
amiably, old friends.
                          *Hi, Jack*—she says.

*Country people*, he thinks, mistakenly.
The routines of home seem a lifetime away
and the scenes of his life rather quaint:
an old genre flick, never quite distinct

enough or strange to be revived
except on TV, and then only very late,

with discount-mattress and hair-transplant ads.

# Green River Cemetery:
## Springs

Strange to be among them in the noon sun
with their fabulous night histories,
the welter and crush of downtown tableaux
above Second Avenue or at the Hotel Earle,
honeycomb of lambent episode.

Big silence in the midday heat
except for insect whir and a passing car:
you imagine them under the sandy ground,
under the slate and granite markers,
and pretend to hear, faintly at first,

as if through the woods at night,
the stream of delicious talk,
the rages, dishing and whispered come-ons,
the posturing and retort
at that murderous cocktail party, the '50s,

Speed and Nerve presiding
right before it blew into a camp B-movie
cavalcade of car wrecks, lithium
and broken hearts
                    (soundtrack by Schoenberg
and Elmer Bernstein). The afterglow of them:
neon on a sunny day—
                    celluloid in flames,
the fried image and random splice,
wild parabolas, butchery.